THE
MARRIAGE PREPARATION COURSE

Leaders' and Support Couples' Guide

Published by Alpha International, Holy Trinity Brompton, Brompton Road, London SW7 1JA.
Email: publications@alpha.org

CONTENTS

Appendices

INTRODUCTION

We have been running *The Marriage Preparation Course* at Holy Trinity Brompton since 1985. During that time the course has changed and developed. We started with a few couples in our home and now hold the course 3 times a year with around 120 engaged couples on each course.

The best time to start supporting couples is right at the beginning, before they marry. In today's climate, with so much marital breakdown, more people are aware of the need to prepare. The choice to marry, no longer an assumption in our society, presents a key moment for learning. Our experience has shown us that many couples are open to receiving help as they approach this lifelong commitment and that they enjoy the experience of learning more about marriage and about their fiancé(e). This is what two couples, who completed the course, said a year or so into their marriage:

> 'The Marriage Preparation Course *was invaluable to us as a couple. Although we had been going out together for four and a half years and thought we knew everything there was to know about each other, we learnt so much and have benefited from it immensely. The testimonies from other married couples have really stuck with us and help even today. On top of that we thoroughly enjoyed each evening.'*

> 'We found that many issues we'd never thought about discussing came up when we did *Marriage Prep. Our relationship has deepened and our expectations of marriage and of each other are even greater and more exciting than they were before. We thoroughly enjoyed the course and gained so much practical advice from it that I believe we will use for years to come!'*

The course is now available for others to use, whether in a large group, or with one or two couples at home. Some groups prefer to use the videos/DVDs to run the course, while others like to give the talks themselves. Whichever you prefer, this manual will help you.

We now run the course in conjunction with the FOCCUS questionnaire and support couples and have found this to be an excellent combination to prepare couples for marriage (see Section D for more details), but the course can be run without these elements and no mention is made of FOCCUS on the videos/DVDs.

We hope that you enjoy using *The Marriage Preparation Course* and that it is a blessing to you and to the couples who attend.

Nicky and Sila Lee

A. WHAT IS INVOLVED?

1) The aim of the course

The aim of *The Marriage Preparation Course* is to provide engaged couples with the tools to build a healthy marriage that will last a lifetime.

Over five evenings spent together they will:

- learn how to make a marriage work

- consider the importance of commitment

- have the opportunity to recognise their differences

- learn the skills necessary for their relationship to develop and grow

- discuss how to nurture their friendship

- learn about listening and expressing feelings, spending time together and resolving conflict

- understand how to make each other feel loved

- discuss how to develop their sexual relationship

- recognise the importance of talking about their goals, values and dreams.

Their privacy as an engaged couple is always respected. There is no requirement to disclose anything personal to a third party. But they are given plenty of opportunities to talk to their fiancé(e) during the discussion times.

2) The guests

The Marriage Preparation Course is for any engaged couple who want to give their marriage the best possible start. The length of their engagement does not matter and they may or may not have fixed a wedding date. While the course emphasises and explains the unique nature of marriage, we welcome couples who are living together and who are wanting to explore marriage.

Although the course is based on Christian principles and is led by Christians, it is suitable for those with no Christian faith or church background and couples do not need to be getting married in a church to come on the course. Over half the people who do the course at Holy Trinity Brompton are not regular churchgoers and, from the feedback we have received, they find the course very helpful. They are not required to do or say anything that would conflict with their own beliefs. But they are given the opportunity to reflect on their core values and to consider how a shared faith strengthens a marriage. For some people it has provided the first contact with the church and a number of couples have gone on to do the Alpha course.[1]

Of course, many guests are Christians who are planning a church wedding, and the course enables them to reflect on the part their faith will play in their marriage as well as to acquire the practical tools needed to build their relationship.

3) The design of the course

The course takes place over five evenings and is best run over five weeks (although the material can be fitted in over a weekend or two Saturdays). The evening sessions start at 7pm with a meal and finish by 9:45pm at the latest.

Each session consists of a meal followed by short talks interspersed with exercises and questions for each couple to discuss. The course is designed to allow the couple as much time as possible to talk through the issues raised during the session. Each evening a married couple is interviewed and asked what they have learned about marriage, particularly regarding the topics for that session.

4) The set-up of the room (see Appendix 1)

The environment is crucial to the success of the course. Attention to detail is important and greatly appreciated by the couples. The room is set up before the guests arrive. The atmosphere needs to be warm and welcoming so that the couples feel that we value them and their relationship.

[1] The Alpha Course is a 15-session practical introduction to the Christian faith designed primarily for non-churchgoers and new Christians

The lighting is kept low and music is played both during the meal and whilst the couples are doing the exercises and talking with their fiancé(e). See Appendix 2 for examples of suitable music.

The room is arranged with tables, tablecloths, table napkins and candles, with three or four engaged couples around each table. There needs to be sufficient space for each couple's conversations to remain private. Background music during the discussion times also helps to ensure privacy.

The set-up may be different for smaller courses being run in a home.

5) The structure of an evening

The evening, including the meal, lasts for up to two hours and forty-five minutes.

Welcome: Guests are welcomed warmly by the leaders. A drink is served and the couples are introduced informally to one another. If the course has more than five or six couples, name badges are helpful.

The meal (30 minutes): This contributes to the effect of the whole evening. Guests sit with at least two other engaged couples. This is the opportunity for engaged couples to meet each other. We work out in advance who goes with whom according to where they live and their ages and experience of life.

There is a main course only because coffee, tea and dessert are served later in the evening during one of the discussions. Many couples have commented that the meal has made the evening special for them and has given them a chance to relax together after work.

Notices and review (5 minutes): After the welcome and notices (if any), the couples are given the opportunity to review the topics covered in the previous session(s).

Talks and discussion:
Throughout this guide, instructions in white boxes relate to courses on which the talks are given by live speakers. Tinted boxes relate to courses on which the course DVDs are used.

Live talks: Short talks are interspersed with exercises and times of discussion for each couple to do on their own. The couples stay at their tables for the talks and their discussions, although they do not discuss anything with another couple. The talks may also be illustrated with DVD reports, street interviews and short one to two minute interviews which are available on a separate DVD titled *The Marriage Preparation Course Inserts*. *The Marriage Preparation Course* CD-ROM contains sample talk transcripts which can be personalised. These transcripts also show where the reports and interviews fit.

DVD: The DVDs include instructions of when and for how long to stop the tape to give couples the opportunity to do the exercises. The length of the exercises varies between five and fifteen minutes.

Interview:

Live talks: Each evening a married couple is interviewed for around five minutes about what has been important in their own relationship, particularly with regard to the topics covered on that session. The recorded interview on the DVD could be used instead.

DVD: A five-minute interview is provided for each week, as well as the shorter interviews with the 'sofa couples' on the topics under discussion.

Concluding remarks and prayer:

Live talks: Each session finishes with a reading of one of the passages from the Bible suggested as a possibility for the wedding service (see Appendix IV of *The Marriage Preparation Course Guest Manual*) followed by a short prayer. The recorded readings on the DVD could be used instead.

DVD: The reading and prayer are provided for you, if you wish to use them.

B. SETTING UP A COURSE

1) Course leaders

The course is best led by a Christian couple who have the desire to help engaged couples build a marriage that will last a lifetime. They should have the support of their church leader. They will need to have some experience of leading groups and a willingness to share openly from their own marriage if they are giving the talks themselves.

There should be no major unresolved issues between them when they start to lead the course and they must both be committed to continuing to build their own marriage. For this reason we recommend that leaders should first do *The Marriage Course* (an eight-session course designed for married couples to strengthen their relationship) before leading *The Marriage Preparation Course*.

2) Professional help

The leaders need to have identified counsellors in their locality to whom they would be happy to refer couples or individuals should issues arise that are beyond their own experience and training.

For large courses a list of counsellors should be available, specifying each counsellor's area of expertise, whether or not they are Christians, how much (if anything) they charge and how to make contact with them.

3) Taskforce

The taskforce supports all aspects of the course including:

- setting up the room
- preparing the meal
- serving the meal
- clearing and washing up

- helping to serve tea and coffee

- music and audio visual support.

The number of helpers required on the taskforce will depend on the size of the course. Even with a course of two or three couples, the leaders will benefit from having others who can help them with the logistics of the food and drink so that they are free to give their full attention to the guests.

On the second and subsequent courses, guests from the previous course are invited to help on the taskforce. Many couples are glad of the opportunity to give something back as well as to hear some of the talks again.

4) Resources required

- A copy of this guide for each leader

- A manual for each of the guests (ie two per couple)

- The course DVD set (either to help the leaders with preparation for live talks or to use with the engaged couples)

- Spare set(s) of audio CDs for couples who miss an evening

- *The Marriage Book* by Nicky and Sila Lee (Alpha International, 2000). Each couple receives a copy of the book on the first evening. The cost is included in the cost of the course

- Music (suitable music is suggested in Appendix 2)

- Tables and chairs

- Tablecloths, candles, candleholders and table napkins

- Cooking, coffee and tea making facilities

- Equipment for playing the DVDs

- Lectern or other stand for speakers' notes.

5) Preparation for each session

The course can be done with the DVDs or by giving the talks live (or by using a combination of these methods). The DVDs clearly indicate when and for how long to pause for each exercise. If doing their own talks the leaders will need to look at the timetable for each evening to know when to stop for the exercises and discussions (see Section C).

If you are giving the talks yourself, start your preparation at least one week beforehand. The speakers' notes are available on *The Marriage Preparation Course* CD-ROM. These notes also contain the timelines for each session. The speakers' notes may be adapted to include illustrations from your own marriage and may be shortened.

It is important that husband and wife share the speaking in order to give both a male and female perspective and also to reinforce the biblical view of complementarity. You may find that one of you feels more drawn to the theory and the other to the practical outworking of it. Allocate the speaking according to gifts and personality.

The following will be helpful in preparing to lead the evening together if you are giving your own talks as a couple:

- Start your preparation with a prayer

- Watch the DVD of that session and read the relevant section of *The Marriage Book* (see Section C for which section of the book relates to each session of the course)

- Talk through the issues raised in the session and any concerns you have

- Decide who will do each section of the talks

- Work out what you are going to use from your own experience. Go through this with each other to make sure that you are agreed about what you will say. Do not include anything that would offend, belittle or upset your husband or wife

- Adjust the speakers' notes (if using the CD-ROM), adding your own illustrations

- Make sure you feel comfortable with the material and are familiar with the exercises

- Prepare the couple giving the testimony. Ideally they should be in their first few years of marriage so that the engaged couples can relate more easily to their experience. The main aim of the testimony is to illustrate the points made in the talks. The testimony should last about five minutes. Choose couples who are willing to be honest and specific and who can add humour to the evening. Both the husband and wife should be interviewed and asked questions that will keep the testimony personal and relevant to the engaged couples. Alternatively leaders may choose to use the testimonies from the *Inserts* DVD.

6) Feedback

A questionnaire has been developed to be distributed on the last evening (see Appendix 3). This serves as a review of the course for the guests and provides helpful feedback for the leaders to know how to make the course more effective the next time. You can print this from the CD-ROM.

The questionnaire can also provide useful quotes to promote the course. These comments should be kept anonymous unless the engaged couple gives permission for their names to be used.

7) Promotion of the course

The message
Whatever the setting, the message to the engaged couples is the same: 'Make the best start to your marriage by preparing for it'. We make it clear that any couple is welcome whether or not they are members of a church. We also assure them that they will not be required to talk about their relationship to anybody else, but that there will be plenty of opportunities to discuss important issues with each other.

Invitations to the course, with the information given above, the dates of the next course and an outline of the topics covered, should be made as widely available as possible (see Appendix 4 for a sample invitation). They could be displayed in church, at register offices, in health centres and at events likely to attract engaged couples. The more invitations in circulation the better.

Most couples come on the course at Holy Trinity Brompton through the recommendation of another couple who has previously completed the course. Once couples from outside the church start to attend and enjoy it, they spread the message to their friends.

Working with other churches

You may want to work together with other local churches to provide preparation for couples planning to get married in church. You will need to gain the support of the other churches and together create a plan for the publicity and running of the course. This approach encourages local co-operation and sharing of resources. One larger course may initially attract more attention than several small ones and draw in couples not planning to marry in a church.

Community Family Policies

A number of places in the UK have started to run 'Community Family Policies'. These policies bring together clergy, teachers, doctors, health visitors and others working in the community to encourage people to invest in their relationships through attending marriage, parenting and marriage preparation courses.

Some Community Family Policies have led to an agreement among the clergy in the area that they will require all the couples they are marrying to attend a marriage preparation course.

Registering a course

If you are planning to run *The Marriage Preparation Course*, please let us know at Holy Trinity Brompton, Brompton Road, London SW7 1JA or via our website at themarriagecourse.org. This will enable us to support you in the future and direct any enquiring engaged couples in your area to your course. We can also advertise your course on the website if you would like us to. Eventually we hope there will be enough courses listed so that any engaged couple wanting to attend can find one within reach of where they live.

C. AN OVERVIEW AND TIMETABLE FOR EACH EVENING

Session 1 – Communication

1) Overview

Effective communication is essential for a strong marriage. This session considers how communication is affected by personality, family background and circumstances. Couples look at what it means to talk about their feelings and they practise listening to each other.

2) Resources

The Marriage Book – Section 2

The Marriage Preparation Course CD-ROM

The Marriage Preparation Course Inserts DVD

The Marriage Preparation Course DVD, Session 1

The Marriage Preparation Course CD, Session 1

3) Checklist

Manual for each guest
Music during: the meal
                 the exercises and discussions
Name labels (if the number of couples warrants them)
Cold drink on arrival
The meal
Tea, coffee and dessert

Tables, tablecloths and chairs

Table napkins, candles and candleholders

Spare pens

Table with recommended books (see Appendix 5)

> Speakers' stand (for large courses)

Guest attendance list

> For live talks, an issue to use in the leaders' demonstration of effective listening (this is needed for Session 1 only)

4) Timetable

The timing for the length of each talk is approximate – time allowed for the exercises should not be shortened.

From 6:30pm Be ready!

Guests often arrive early on the first evening

Welcome and offer a drink

7:00pm Meal

Main course only

7:30pm Notices

- Please write your name on your manual

- Let us know in good time if you can't come for one of the evenings and we will give/send you the CD

- Relax! There is no group work. Many people have two fears about coming on a course like this. One is that they will be required to talk to others about their relationship. The other is that their fiancé(e) might talk to strangers about their relationship!

- We put you in a group over supper to give you the opportunity to meet one or two other engaged couples.

Icebreaker

This part is entirely optional and is designed to help everyone get to know another couple better. You may ask the couples to tell another couple they are sitting with:

- when they are getting married

- where they first met (there may be two versions for this!).

DVD: Play the DVD. Session 1 lasts for 48 minutes, but in addition you will need to allow 40 minutes for the exercises:

- How we communicate – allow 5 minutes

- Family styles of communication – allow 10 minutes
  (during which drinks and dessert are served)

- Effective talking – allow 10 minutes

- Effective listening – allow 15 minutes

This means the whole session takes **1 hour 28 minutes.**

Live talks:

7:40pm	**Talk:** The value of marriage preparation
8:00pm	**Discussion** (if using FOCCUS questionnaire) 'Spend a few minutes asking your support couple any questions you may have about the FOCCUS questionnaire'
8:05pm	**Talk:** Learning to communicate
8:15pm	**Exercise:** How we communicate
8:20pm	**Talk:** Learning to communicate (cont)
8:25pm	**Exercise:** Family styles of communication (during which coffee, tea and dessert are served to the engaged couples by the leaders and support couples)
8:35pm	**Talk:** Learning to communicate (cont)

8:45pm	**Testimony:** By a married couple who talk about their own experience of learning to communicate effectively in their marriage (or show testimony on DVD)
8:50pm	**Exercise:** Effective talking
9:00pm	**Talk:** Learning to communicate (cont)
9:10pm	**Leaders' demonstration of effective listening:** Before the evening, one of you needs to have thought of an issue that is bothering you that you have not previously discussed. Do not choose an issue that would be hurtful or embarrassing to your husband or wife.
	Model the steps for effective listening in the exercise in the guest manual
9:15pm	**Exercise:** Effective listening
9:30pm	**Conclusion**

- 'The homework is not the sort we take in and mark! It is designed to help you to follow up the topic of that (or the next) session on your own'

- We will finish each evening by reading one of the passages suggested as a possibility for your marriage service in Appendix IV of *The Marriage Preparation Course Guest Manual*

- Read Colossians 3:12–17 (or show reading on *Inserts* DVD)

- Close the session with a short prayer eg 'Lord, thank you that you are the God of love. Thank you that you always listen to us. Please help us to put on love and to be good at listening to each other. Amen.'

Session 2 – Commitment

1) Overview

Commitment lies at the heart of the marriage covenant and is reflected in the marriage service vows. Couples consider the meaning of these vows and then look at how to live out this commitment through making quality time for each other on a regular basis and separating appropriately from their parents.

2) Resources

The Marriage Book – Sections 1 and 6 and Epilogue (Chapter 20)

The Marriage Preparation Course CD-ROM

The Marriage Preparation Course Inserts DVD

The Marriage Preparation Course DVD, Session 2

The Marriage Preparation Course CD, Session 2

3) Checklist

As for Session 1

Two sheets of differently coloured paper and two sheets of differently coloured paper which have been stuck together with glue.

Spare guest manuals

4) Timetable

From 6:45pm
Welcome guests with a drink

7:00pm Meal
Main course only

7:30pm Notices and review

- 'Please bring your manuals for each session – there are spare ones to borrow for any who have forgotten theirs. Please use the blank paper for writing on and then transfer anything you write into your own manual'

- 'Tell your fiancé(e) what you realised about marriage on Session 1. Look back in your manual to be reminded of what was covered'

DVD: Play the DVD. Session 2 lasts for 54 minutes, but in addition you will need to allow 40 minutes for the exercises:

- The benefits of marriage – allow 5 minutes

- The marriage vows – allow 10 minutes

- Planning time together – allow 15 minutes (during which drinks and dessert are served)

- Parents and in-laws – allow 10 minutes

This means the whole session takes **1 hour 34 minutes.**

Live talks: Timings

7:40pm	**Talk:** Why marriage?
7:55pm	**Exercise:** The benefits of marriage
8:00pm	**Talk:** The marriage covenant
8:10pm	**Exercise:** The marriage vows
8:20pm	**Talk:** Spending time together
8:45pm	**Exercise:** Planning time together (during which coffee, tea and dessert are served)
9:00pm	**Talk:** The change of loyalties
9:15pm	**Exercise:** Parents and in-laws
9:25pm	**Testimony:** By a married couple who talk about 'marriage time' and developing their relationship with their parents and in-laws
9:30pm	**Conclusion**

- Allowing time apart – this introduces the homework for Session 2

- Read Philippians 2:1–7 (or show reading on *Inserts* DVD)

- End with a short prayer eg 'Lord, thank you for your commitment to us. Thank you that you came to serve us. Please help us to serve each other and to live out our commitment to one another throughout our marriage. Amen.'

Session 3 – Resolving conflict

1) Overview

Conflict can either destroy a marriage or, if handled well, strengthen it. Couples consider how to handle anger, appreciate their differences, look for solutions together and practise forgiveness. Organising finances, a primary cause of conflict in marriage, is also addressed.

2) Resources

The Marriage Book – Sections 4 and 5 and Appendix 3

The Marriage Preparation Course CD-ROM

The Marriage Preparation Course Inserts DVD

The Marriage Preparation Course DVD, Session 3

The Marriage Preparation Course CD, Session 3

3) Checklist

As for Session 1
Spare guest manuals

4) Timetable

From 6:45pm
Welcome guests with a drink

7:00pm Meal
Main course only

7:30pm Review

- Do a short reminder of the main topics covered on Sessions 1 and 2

- 'Ask your fiancé(e) what was most important for them from the last session'

DVD: Play the DVD. Session 3 lasts for 55 minutes, but in addition you will need to allow 40 minutes for the exercises:

- Rhinos and hedgehogs? – allow 5 minutes

- Look at your differences – allow 10 minutes

- Using the six steps – allow 15 minutes (during which drinks and dessert are served)

- Discussing your finances – allow 10 minutes

This means the whole session takes **1 hour 35 minutes.**

Live talks:

7:40pm   **Talk:** Expecting conflict and handling anger

7:50pm   **Exercise:** Rhinos and hedgehogs

7:55pm   **Talk:** Accepting our differences

8:10pm   **Exercise:** Look at your differences

8:20pm   **Talk:** Looking for solutions

8:35pm   **Exercise:** Using the six steps
                (during which coffee, tea and dessert are served)

8:50pm   **Talk:** Dealing with finances

9:00pm   **Exercise:** Discussing your finances

9:10pm   **Talk:** Forgiving each other

9:25pm   **Testimony:** By a married couple who talk about the effect of the differences between them on their marriage and what has been important for them in resolving conflict

9:30pm   **Conclusion**

- Read 1 Corinthians 13:4–8 (or show reading on *Inserts* DVD)

- End with a short prayer eg 'Thank you Lord that you are so patient and so kind towards us. Thank you that you forgive us. Please fill us with your love. Help us to forgive each other and to keep no record of each other's wrongs. Amen.'

Session 4 – Keeping love alive

1) Overview

Love must be deliberately nurtured in a marriage. Couples do this through nurturing their friendship, discovering how the other feels loved and developing their sexual relationship.

2) Resources

The Marriage Book – Sections 3 and 7 and Appendix 2

The Marriage Preparation Course CD-ROM

The Marriage Preparation Course Inserts DVD

The Marriage Preparation Course DVD, Session 4

The Marriage Preparation Course CD, Session 4

3) Checklist

As for Session 1
Spare guest manuals

4) Timetable

From 6:45pm
Welcome guests with a drink

7:00pm Meal
Main course only

7:30pm Review

- Do a short reminder of the main topics covered on Sessions 1–3

- 'Ask your fiancé(e) what was most important for them from the last session'

DVD: Play the video or DVD. Session 4 lasts for 58 minutes, but in addition, you will need to allow 40 minutes for the exercises:

- Building friendship – allow 10 minutes

- Discover your 'love languages' – allow 10 minutes (during which drinks and dessert are served)

- Sex and commitment – allow 10 minutes

- Talking about sex – allow 10 minutes

This means the whole session takes **1 hour 38 minutes**.

Live talks:

7:40pm	**Talk:** Developing our friendship
7:50pm	**Exercise:** Building friendship
8:00pm	**Talk:** Discovering each other's needs
8:15pm	**Exercise:** Discover your 'love languages'
8:25pm	**Talk:** Building our sexual relationship
8:45pm	**Exercise:** Sex and commitment (during which coffee, tea and dessert are served)
8:55pm	**Talk:** How to build your sexual relationship
9:15pm	**Exercise:** Talking about sex
9:25pm	**Testimony:** By a married couple who talk about their own experience of the topics covered
9:30pm	**Conclusion**

- Read Song of Songs 8:6–7 and Psalm 85:10–13 (or show reading on *Inserts* DVD)

- End with a short prayer eg 'Thank you Lord for the wonderful gift of sexual intimacy. We ask you to teach us how to use this gift to express and to receive love. And we pray that, in each marriage and future marriage represented here, love and faithfulness would meet together. Amen.'

Session 5 – Shared goals and values

1) Overview

While appreciating their differences, couples need to agree on their goals and core values. They have the opportunity to discuss their priorities for the future, the roles they each expect to fulfil and the building of spiritual togetherness.

2) Resources

The Marriage Book – Chapter 10 and Appendix 4

The Marriage Preparation Course CD-ROM

The Marriage Preparation Course Inserts DVD

The Marriage Preparation Course DVD, Session 5

The Marriage Preparation Course CD, Session 5

3) Checklist

As for Session 1
Spare guest manuals
The Marriage Preparation Course questionnaires (one per guest) – see Appendix 3
Invitations to the next *Marriage Preparation Course*
Invitations to *The Marriage Course*
Invitations to the Alpha course

4) Timetable

From 6:45pm
Welcome guests with a drink

7:00pm Meal
(main course only)

7:30pm Notices

- Encourage guests to take invitations to the next *Marriage Preparation Course* to give to friends who are engaged

- Encourage them to take invitations to *The Marriage Course* to give away to friends who are already married. Explain that the content and format of *The Marriage Course* is similar to this course but it is designed for married couples and that more time is spent on some of the topics. Recommend they do *The Marriage Course* themselves two years or so into their marriage, or sooner if they feel the need to

- Explain that the Alpha course is for anyone who wants to explore the Christian faith. We are looking in this session at the difference that a joint faith can make to a marriage. Alpha is a good way of discussing spiritual issues together. Say there are invitations on the book table and they would be very welcome to come to the next course on their own or together as a couple

- Ask them each to fill in *The Marriage Preparation Course* questionnaire. This serves two purposes. First it is a good reminder for them of the topics we have covered on the course. It therefore acts as the 'review' on this session. Secondly it is a great help to us in developing the course for other engaged couples. We ask them to answer as honestly as they can and we give them a few minutes at the end to make comments on this final session.

DVD: Play the DVD. Session 5 lasts for 54 minutes, but in addition you will need to allow 40 minutes for the exercises:

- Expressing appreciation – allow 10 minutes

- Living out your values – allow 15 minutes (during which drinks and dessert are served)

- Roles and responsibilities – allow 10 minutes

- Spiritual togetherness – allow 5 minutes

This means the whole session takes **1 hour 34 minutes.**

Live talks:

7:45pm   **Talk:** Matching our strides

8:00pm   **Exercise:** Expressing appreciation

8:10pm	**Talk:** Working out our values
8:30pm	**Exercise:** Living out your values (during which coffee, tea and dessert are served)
8:45pm	**Talk:** Creating an equal partnership
9:00pm	**Exercise:** Roles and responsibilities
9:10pm	**Talk:** Building spiritual togetherness
9:20pm	**Exercise:** Spiritual togetherness
9:25pm	**Testimony:** By a married couple who talk about how they have worked out different roles in their own marriage and the difference it makes to them to have a common faith and/or to pray with and for each other
9:30pm	**Conclusion**

- Read 1 John 4:7–8; 13–19 (or show reading on *Inserts* DVD)

- End with a short prayer eg 'Lord, thank you that we can know and rely on the love that you have for us. Please bless every couple here in their love for each other. May their marriage be a source of great joy and encouragement to them and to many others. We ask that you guard and strengthen their relationship, and help them to build a marriage that lasts a lifetime. We ask this in Jesus' name. Amen.'

D. FOCCUS AND SUPPORT COUPLE TRAINING NOTES

FOCCUS[2]

FOCCUS is a psychometric inventory designed to facilitate open and honest communication between a couple. It is not an essential element of *The Marriage Preparation Course* and is not available in every country. However, we have found it to be extremely valuable in helping couples to identify issues they need to discuss and to give them an opportunity to discuss these issues with a support couple (see below).

We encourage engaged couples to complete FOCCUS before starting the course so that the issues we address have already been raised in their minds (and have sometimes led to discussions between them).

We recommend that you run your first few *Marriage Preparation Courses* without FOCCUS and then, if you can, introduce it when you feel confident with the material. More information can be found at the FOCCUS website: www.foccusinc.com.

The course may also be used in conjunction with other questionnaires such as PREPARE.[3]

Support couples

The support couples are married couples who act as hosts for each evening. During the course or soon afterwards the engaged couples meet their support couple on their own to discuss their FOCCUS questionnaire results and other issues that may have arisen as a result of doing the course.This normally takes place in the support couple's home.

---

[2] The FOCCUS questionnaire was created by Dr Barbara Markey, FOCCUS Inc., 3214 N. 60th Street, Omaha, NE 68104-3495, USA, Tel: 402-877-882-5422, Website: www.foccusinc.com
In the UK the FOCCUS materials can be obtained from Nicholas Gulliford, Quel Bec, Cothelstone, Taunton TA1 3ED, Tel: 01823 432 420, Email: info@affinities.org.uk

[3] The PREPARE questionnaire was created by Drs David Olson, John Druckman and David Fournier, Life Innovations Inc., PO Box 190 Minneapolis, MN 55440-0190, USA. If you are in the UK and you want to find out more about how to incorporate PREPARE with *The Marriage Preparation Course*, contact john.deagle@tesco.net (Tel: 07803 903490)

The support couple's aim is to encourage the engaged couples to express their thoughts and feelings openly and honestly to each other within the framework of a listening and loving environment. We match the support couples and engaged couples by where they live and, as far as possible, by age (so that the engaged couple is not older than the support couple).

Support couples will not have flawless marriages but need to be willing to share their own experiences and the realities of marriage from a personal perspective. They are not counsellors. They come alongside the engaged couple to discuss issues in a non-judgmental and non-prescriptive manner. They know that if an issue comes up that is beyond their own knowledge and experience, they are able to refer the couple on for more specialised help.

The support couples are drawn mainly from *The Marriage Course*. During the notices at the start of the sixth session of *The Marriage Course*, we describe *The Marriage Preparation Course* and the role of the support couples. We ask couples who are interested to make contact with us and then describe in more detail what it involves. We ask for a reference from someone with pastoral oversight if we do not know them well ourselves. If they have enough experience of marriage (at least two years) and are suitable, we invite them to an initial training evening (see training notes below). We have produced an audio tape for any couple who misses this training.

The combination of *The Marriage Course* and this training is sufficient for them to start helping on the next *Marriage Preparation Course*.

Support couple training notes
1) Introduction to the FOCCUS questionnaire

- FOCCUS stands for 'Facilitating Open Couple Communication, Understanding and Study'

- The questionnaire can either be completed online or on paper and the results sent away for computer analysis

- Couples answer 156 questions on their own with '*Agree*', '*Disagree*' or '*Uncertain*'. (They answer additional questions if they are cohabiting/

interfaith/on their second or subsequent marriage.) See Appendix 6 for sample questions

- Having both completed the questionnaire, the couples are free to discuss the questions with each other (This accounts for 40 per cent of the benefit of doing the questionnaire.)

- Their answers are analysed and compared through a computer program to reveal the areas that require discussion, either because they have different understandings to each other or because their answers are different to the author's 'preferred answer'

- The couples meet up with a support couple to discuss the results

- The aims of the questionnaire are:

  i.   for the couple to explore all issues that require discussion
  ii. for the couple to be sure they are ready for marriage
  iii. for the couple to have a realistic view of what makes a strong marriage.

- The questionnaire is not a test of compatibility.

2) How to interpret the results

(See Appendix 7 for sample page)

- The questions are grouped into nineteen sections (including the three for interfaith, remarriage and cohabiting couples to be filled in if relevant)

- Some questions will appear in more than one section

- Percentage of agreement 75 per cent and above generally represent areas of strength in a relationship

- Percentage of agreement 40 per cent and below generally represent areas that deserve special attention

- Look for the lowest percentage agreement to see which sections will require most discussion

- Each section shows which questions are 'key problem indicators' – these are regarded as basic to a healthy marriage. They are also summarised separately.

3) How to facilitate discussion

The aim

- Marriage support:

  - IS NOT lecturing

  - IS NOT counselling

  - IS facilitating discussion

  - IS sharing personal experience when appropriate.

- The main aim of the support couple is to facilitate conversation between the couple, helping them to listen to each other, to share thoughts and feelings and, if necessary, to work for solutions and compromises

- The main skill is listening and guiding their discussion.

Your preparation

- Prepare carefully beforehand, deciding which sections to cover and choosing the questions in those sections to look at with the couple (one or two questions per section are often sufficient)

- Use the 'FOCCUS feedback form' to write down areas and particular questions for discussion (see Appendix 8)

- Decide which roles each of you best fulfils to facilitate discussion (ie one of you may be better at asking the initial questions, the other better at listening and picking up hidden assumptions)

- Pray together before the engaged couple arrives.

The discussion

- Take time to get to know the couple first – perhaps by talking over a simple meal (lasting no more than about forty minutes) or over dessert and coffee

- Allow one and a half to two hours to discuss the FOCCUS results

- Work out how you are going to sit (a three-seater sofa or two chairs angled towards each other so the engaged couple can address each other is ideal)

- If they are Christians, pray for the couple and for your time together before looking at the results

- You might like to give them a copy of the questionnaire (see footnote on page 25 for where these may be obtained)

- Ask them if doing the questionnaire has already led to helpful conversations

- Look at the results graph with the couple only if you feel this will be helpful for them (see Appendix 7 for sample)

- Otherwise look at the different sections in the 'FOCCUS feedback form' to show them the different areas (see Appendix 8)

- Talk about the section(s) with a high percentage agreement first in order to encourage them

- Move to the section with the lowest percentage agreement and look at an item of disagreement, uncertainty or non-preferred answer

- Say to one of them: '*Do you remember how you responded to question X? Tell your fiance(é) why you put that answer.*' (Some areas of disagreement will no longer be relevant as they will already have discussed and resolved the issue.)

- This may start a spontaneous conversation between them. Or you may need to ask the other one, '*What do you think?*' or, '*How does that make you feel?*'

- Supplementary questions for each area are available in the 'FOCCUS facilitator notebook'

- If they ask for help or guidance, don't give them your answer too quickly. Ask them to state what they think the problem/issue really is for them, so they 'own' the question for themselves. Then be willing to share from your own experience and suggest strategies you have found helpful in your own marriage

- Do not feel you have to cover every question over which they disagree. Choosing one or two key items for discussion in a given section often covers the whole area

- Leave enough time to ask if there is anything else that they would like to discuss

- Invite them back for another session if you feel that is necessary

- If they are Christians ask if they would like you to pray for them before they go. Couples who are not involved in a church often appreciate this offer but should feel completely free to decline

- Have an Alpha invitation to give them if they express an interest in exploring spiritual issues further

- Give them the 'FOCCUS feedback form' (Appendix 8) to take away with them, indicating further areas or questions for them to discuss on their own. You can print this from the CD-ROM

- If this is the last (or only) meeting with the couple, destroy your copy of their results.

4) Dealing with sensitive issues

- If you feel out of your depth with any issues that come up in your discussions, do not be afraid to tell the couple that this area is beyond your own experience. Ask them if they would like you to refer them for more specialised help. If so ask the course leader(s) how to proceed

- Cohabitation – this is addressed in Session 4 of the course. Respond to their questions and concerns rather than initiating your own opinions

- Homosexuality – if this is revealed by one or other of them through the questionnaire as an area they are concerned about, help them to express this to each other. If they want more guidance and support which is beyond your own abilities, ask the course leaders where to refer them for more specialised help

- High levels of disagreement – the issue is not whether you think they are wise to be getting married. Your time with them will draw out the areas of difference/disagreement and help them decide as they reflect on the important issues

- Addictions – marriage itself will not automatically lead to changes in behaviour. The couple needs to understand that they will not be able to change each other after marriage. Your discussion might help them to be realistic about the effect of any addictive behaviour on their relationship. Refer them for more specialised help if they request this

- Uncertainty about marriage – the course, the questionnaire and your time with them will all help either to reinforce their doubts and fears or to lessen them. We may need them to help distinguish between a fear of commitment (marriage takes courage) and a fear that they are marrying the wrong person. Of course, the decision about whether or not to marry is theirs, not ours. See *The Marriage Book* Appendix 1 for the 'Seven tests of love'

- Pre-nuptial agreements – the most important issue is not what we think about such agreements, but whether the couple is in agreement with each other. If one of them is trying to persuade the other to sign, this can lead to resentment and an underlying lack of trust at the start of the marriage. Our role is to help them express their feelings to each other.

5) Why couples should not keep the questionnaire or results

- The report is not a permanent measure of the couple's relationship

- It is a snapshot at a moment in time – simple discussion can move them on quickly. Their scores will almost certainly have changed through doing the course

- It is a tool for discussion and not a weapon to be used against each other in the future

- It is designed for use with a support couple

- The couple can find out everything from each other anyway

- The 'FOCCUS feedback form' is more helpful for them to keep and is all that they need

- If the couple is insistent, please ask them to talk to the course leaders.

APPENDIX 1 – SUGGESTED ROOM SET-UP FOR EIGHTEEN COUPLES

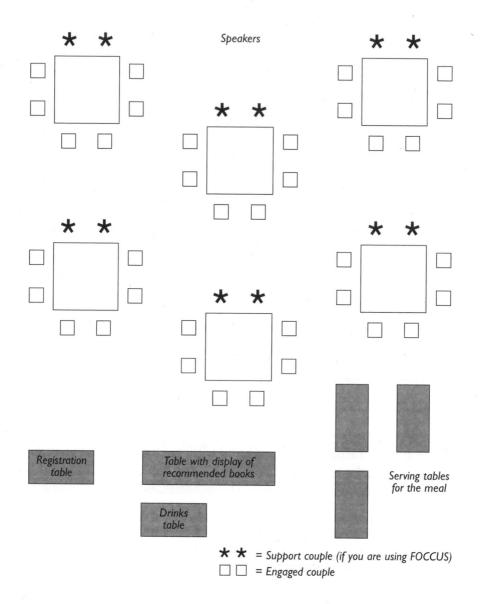

Speakers

Registration table

Table with display of recommended books

Drinks table

Serving tables for the meal

★ ★ = Support couple (if you are using FOCCUS)
☐ ☐ = Engaged couple

APPENDIX 2 – EXAMPLES OF SUITABLE MUSIC

Session 1

During the meal:
Ella Fitzgerald and Louis Armstrong, *Ella and Louis* (Verve, 1956 and 2000)

During the exercises and discussions:
Norah Jones, *Come Away With Me* (EMI, 2002)

Session 2

During the meal:
Steven Curtis Chapman, *For the One I Love* (StraightWay Music, 1997)

During the exercises and discussions:
Eva Cassidy, *Songbird* (Blix Street Records, 1998)

Session 3

During the meal:
Charlie Haden & Pat Metheny, *Beyond the Missouri Sky* (Polydor/Polygram, 1997)

During the exercises and discussions:
Natalie Merchant, *Tigerlily* (Elektra, 1995)

Session 4

During the meal:
Enya, *Shepherd Moons* (Warner Music, 1991)

During the exercises and discussions:
Sara Groves, *Conversations* (PW Music, 2000)

Session 5

During the meal:
Iona, *Open Sky* (Alliance Music, 2000)

During the exercises and discussions:
Maire Brennan, *Perfect Time* (Word Records, 1998)

APPENDIX 3

THE
MARRIAGE
PREPARATION
COURSE

This questionnaire is a great help to us in developing the course. Please answer as thoroughly as you can. Your answers will remain anonymous.

Name: (optional)

How long have you been engaged?

How did you hear about The Marriage Preparation Course?

Are you a member of a church? Yes / No

If so, which one?

In what ways, if any, has the course helped to prepare you for marriage?

What were the most important things you learnt on the course?

What did you enjoy most about the course?

What did you find most difficult?

Did you have any difficulties completing FOCCUS on the internet? Yes / No

If yes, please explain:

Did you benefit from doing the FOCCUS questionnaire? Yes / No

Please explain:

Did you benefit from going through FOCCUS with your support couple (if you have seen them)? Yes / No

Please explain:

Please indicate how helpful each section of the course was to you by circling a number, or leave blank if not applicable.

PLEASE CIRCLE 1 – 5 (1 = 'Not helpful' to 5 = 'Invaluable')

		TOPIC					
Session 1 **Communication**		*The value of marriage preparation*	1	2	3	4	5
		Learning to communicate & exercises: *Family styles of communication,* *Effective talking* and *Effective listening*	1	2	3	4	5
		Session 1 Homework	1	2	3	4	5
Session 2 **Commitment**		*Why marriage?* & exercise: *The benefits of marriage*	1	2	3	4	5
		The marriage covenant & exercise: *The marriage vows*	1	2	3	4	5
		Spending time together & exercise: *Planning time together*	1	2	3	4	5
		The change of loyalties & exercise: *Parents and in-laws*	1	2	3	4	5
		Session 2 Homework	1	2	3	4	5
Session 3 **Resolving conflict**		*Expecting conflict*	1	2	3	4	5
		Handling anger & exercise: *Rhinos and hedgehogs*	1	2	3	4	5
		Accepting our differences & exercise: *Look at your differences*	1	2	3	4	5
		Looking for solutions & exercise: *Using the six steps*	1	2	3	4	5

Continued . . .

		TOPIC					
Session 3 cont. **Resolving conflict**		Dealing with finances & exercise: Discussing your finances	1	2	3	4	5
		Forgiving each other	1	2	3	4	5
		Session 3 Homework	1	2	3	4	5
Session 4 **Keeping love alive**		Developing our friendship & exercise: Building friendship	1	2	3	4	5
		Discovering each other's needs & exercise: Discover your 'love languages'	1	2	3	4	5
		Building our sexual relationship & exercises: Sex and commitment and Talking about sex	1	2	3	4	5
		Session 4 Homework	1	2	3	4	5
Session 5 **Shared goals & values**		Matching our strides & exercise: Expressing appreciation	1	2	3	4	5
		Working out our values & exercise: Living out our values	1	2	3	4	5
		Creating an equal partnership & exercise: Roles and responsibilities	1	2	3	4	5
		Building spiritual togetherness & exercise: Spiritual togetherness	1	2	3	4	5
		Session 5 Homework	1	2	3	4	5

What other issues could be addressed on the course and how could we improve the course?

Any other comments:

Thank you for your feedback

APPENDIX 4 – THE MARRIAGE PREPARATION COURSE INVITATION

THE MARRIAGE PREPARATION COURSE

Developing strong foundations for a lasting marriage

What is The Marriage Preparation Course?

The Marriage Preparation Course is for any engaged couple who wants to develop strong foundations for a lasting marriage.

Over five evenings spent together you will learn important tools that will enable you to make your marriage work.

You will look at:
- how to recognise and appreciate your differences
- the art of communication
- the importance of commitment
- resolving conflict
- spending time together
- nurturing your friendship
- making each other feel loved
- developing a good sexual relationship
- the importance of talking about your goals, values and dreams

What's involved?

The evenings are very relaxed. There is a meal followed by short talks interspersed with exercises and questions for you to discuss together as a couple. Before the first evening you and your fiancé(e) will be asked to fill in a questionnaire which is confidential and designed to help you learn more about yourselves and your relationship. You will then be given the opportunity to discuss these issues with a support couple if you wish.

Who is it for?

It is for any engaged couple who wants to have the best possible start to their marriage. The course, while based on Christian principles, is very helpful and relevant for any couple with or without a Christian faith or church background.

Alpha

Registration Form

Please fill in this form and send it [with your payment if applicable] to the address overleaf to let us know you are coming

Title	First Name		Title	First Name
Surname			Surname	
Address			Address	
Postcode			Postcode	
Daytime telephone			Daytime telephone	
Email			Email	
Age			Age	
Do you belong to a church? Yes / No			Do you belong to a church? Yes / No	
If yes, please state which church			If yes, please state which church	
Date of wedding (if known)			☐ Payment enclosed ☐ Bursary required	

APPENDIX 5
– RECOMMENDED BOOKS

Gary Chapman, *The Five Love Languages* (Northfield Publishing, 1995)

Gary Chapman, *The Other Side of Love: Handling Anger in a Godly Way*, (Moody Press, 1999)

Dr Henry Cloud and Dr John Townsend, *Boundaries in Marriage* (Zondervan, 1999)

Willard F Harley, *His Needs, Her Needs* (Monarch Books, 2002)

J. John, *Look Before You Leap* (Authentic Publications, 2002)

Nicky and Sila Lee, *The Marriage Book* (Alpha International, 2000)

Mike Mason, *Mystery of Marriage* (Triangle, 1997)

Rob Parsons, *Sixty Minute Marriage* (Hodder & Stoughton, 1997)

Rob Parsons, *Loving Against the Odds* (Hodder & Stoughton, 1997)

Douglas Rosenau, *A Celebration of Sex* (Nelson, 2002)

Stephen Arterburn and Fred Stoeker, *Every Man's Battle* (Waterbrook Press, 2003)

APPENDIX 6 – THE FOCCUS QUESTIONNAIRE – SAMPLE QUESTIONS

A = I agree   D = I disagree   U = I am uncertain

We are in agreement about the roles each of us expects of the other in our relationship	A	D	U
My future partner and I seldom differ in our need to talk things out or keep things to ourselves	A	D	U
I am hoping that after marriage my partner will change some of his/her behaviours	A	D	U
Sometimes my partner feels that I do not listen to him/her	A	D	U
We have discussed the ways our families solve problems and how this may affect our problem solving	A	D	U
We agree on the values and beliefs in which we will raise any children we may have	A	D	U
I am concerned that the past sexual experience could affect our relationship in a negative way	A	D	U
We are in agreement about how we will make financial decisions between us	A	D	U
I sometimes feel that my partner may not be the right person for me to marry	A	D	U
We have discussed and agree on what being faithful will mean in our relationship	A	D	U

The couple fill in their answers without discussing the questions with each other and without seeing what the other has put. There are 156 questions (plus 3 additional sections for remarriage, interfaith and cohabiting couples). Their answers when analysed are grouped under nineteen sections and presented as a graph to show their levels of agreement within each section (see Appendix 7).

APPENDIX 7 – FOCCUS
SAMPLE RESULTS PAGE

An Inventory for Marriage Preparation

© FOCCUS inc. all rights reserved

Facilitator Revd Nicky and Sila [HTB] Lee Tuesday, November 30, 2004 at 17:15:25

Affiliation Alpha/HTB, 25 CofE London Web page themarriagecourse.org/preparation/welcome/whatsinvolved/

Initials	EVE	ADM
Reference	Sample	Sample
Date	15/03/2004	15/03/2004
Age	26	27
Income Before Tax	£15,000 - £19,999	£20,000 - £29,999
Education Completed	Other Higher Education	Overseas/EFL
Religious Preference	None/Other	Jewish/Reform/Liberal
Religious Attendance	Never	Occasional
Marital Status	Cohabiting (single)	Divorced
Race or Ethnic Origin	Mixed/Other	White/Anglo
Months Courting	12	12
Anyone Pregnant ?	N	N
Anyone With Children ?	N	N

Category	Percentage Agreement
Lifestyle Expectations	58%
Friends and Interests	58%
Personality Match	77%
Personal Issues	92%
Summary : match	72%
Communication	86%
Problem Solving	92%
Summary : skills	88%
Beliefs and Values	33%
Parenting Issues	58%
Extended Family Issues	40%
Sexuality Issues	75%
Financial Issues	33%
Readiness Issues	85%
Marriage Covenant	55%
Summary : bonders	55%
Marriage Commitment	68%
Key Problem Indicators	72%
Family of Origin	48%
Dual Careers	52%
Interfaith Couples	33%
Remarriage Couples	45%
Cohabiting Couples	52%

APPENDIX 8 – FOCCUS
FEEDBACK FORM
(Double sided)

FOCCUS Feedback Form

Areas for discussion	Reference in The Marriage Book
Tick here	
Lifestyle expectations Expectations of roles, career goals, style of home etc.	Chapters 1&2 Appendix 1
Tick here	
Friends and interests Shared and individual friends, time together and time alone	Chapter 2
Tick here	
Personality match Recognising and appreciating differences in your personality types	Chapter 5 - 8
Tick here	
Personal issues Personal problem areas such as bad habits, drugs, drink, social behaviour	Appendix 1
Tick here	
Communication Listening and talking, how well you share ideas and feelings with one another	Chapters 3 & 4
Tick here	
Problem solving Recognising attitudes, past experiences and role models for resolving conflict	Chapters 8, 9, 11 & 12
Tick here	
Beliefs and values Shared hope, common values, practising forgiveness, rituals for daily living	Chapter 10 Appendix 4
Tick here	
Parenting issues Fears, hopes and expectations about having children and how to bring them up	Chapters 13 - 15
Tick here	
Extended family issues Striking a healthy balance with present/future interaction with own family and in-laws	Chapters 13 & 14
Tick here	
Sexuality issues Family attitudes, negative experiences, views and expectations	Chapter 16 – 19 Appendix 2
Tick here	
Financial issues Underlying beliefs and values about money, roles, careers and parenting	Chapter 8 Appendix 4

(Reverse side)

Tick here

Readiness issues   *Appendix 1*

How free and realistic is your decision to marry

Tick here

Marriage covenant   *Chapters 10 & 20*

Commitment and faithfulness in both good and difficult times; having God at the centre
of your marriage

Tick here

Marriage commitment   *Chapters 1 & 20*

Giving what it takes to build a marriage: Accommodating change; investing in your
relationship; showing faithfulness

Tick here

Family of origin   *Chapters 13 & 15*

Messages that you received when growing up about marriage as shown in your
thoughts, feelings and actions

Tick here

Dual careers   *Chapters 1 & 2*

Strengths and challenges of both being employed; views about full-time
parenting

Tick here

Interfaith couples   *Chapter 10*
                                                                      Appendix 4

Shared and different religious/spiritual practice and beliefs

Tick here

Remarriage couples   *Chapters 11 & 12*
                                                                      Appendix 3

Effects of past relationships; the combining of households, resources, financial
and child obligations

Tick here

Cohabiting couples   *Chapter 20*

Expectations for marriage; commitment; level of independence; patterns and experiences
from the time of cohabitation

Particular questions from the FOCCUS questionnaire for more discussion